City Safari

Seagull

Isabel Thomas

Heinemann
LIBRARY
Chicago, Illinois

To contact Capstone Global Library please phone 800-747-4992,
or visit our website www.capstonepub.com

Edited by Dan Nunn, Rebecca Rissman, and Helen Cox
Cannons
Designed by Tim Bond
Original illustrations © Capstone Global Library Ltd 2014
Picture research by Mica Brancic
Production by Helen McCreath
Originated by Capstone Global Library Ltd
Printed and bound in China

17 16 15 14 13
10 9 8 7 6 5 4 3 2 1

Library of Congress Cataloging-in-Publication Data
Thomas, Isabel, 1980- author.
  Seagull / Isabel Thomas.
     pages cm.—(City safari)
  Includes bibliographical references and index.
  ISBN 978-1-4329-8810-4 (hb)—ISBN 978-1-4329-8817-3 (pb) 1.
Gulls—Juvenile literature. 2. Gulls—Behavior—Juvenile literature.
3. Urban animals—Juvenile literature. I. Title.

QL696.C46T46 2014
598.3′38—dc23   2013017410

Acknowledgments
The author and publisher are grateful to the following for
permission to reproduce copyright material: Alamy pp. 16
(© Stephen Dorey), 23 scavenge (© Nik Taylor Wildlife); Getty
Images pp. 8 (Gordon Dixon), 10 (Jonathan Daniel), 11 (Taxi
Japan/Hiroshi Watanabe), 17 (Photonica/Tony Cordoza), 23
loaf (Taxi Japan/Hiroshi Watanabe), 23 roost (Jonathan Daniel),
Naturepl.com pp. 5 (2020VISION/© Peter Cairns), 6 (© David
Tipling), 7 (2020VISION/© Terry Whittaker), 12 (© Graham Eaton),
13 (© Michael D. Kern), 14 (© Laurent Geslin), 19 (© David
Tipling), 20 (© Ann & Steve Toon), 21 (© Markus Varesvuo), 23
flock (© Laurent Geslin); Rex Features pp. 18 and 23 mate (both
Splashdown Direct); Shutterstock pp. 4 (© Marcin Wasilewski), 9
(© Elnur), 15 (© MelBrackstone), 23 roadkill (© Valeniker).

Front cover photograph of a seagull reproduced with
permission of Shutterstock (© aaleksander). Back cover
photograph of a seagull eating in a harbour reproduced with
permission of Shutterstock (© Marcin Wasilewski).

We would like to thank Michael Bright for his invaluable help in
the preparation of this book.

Every effort has been made to contact copyright holders of any
material reproduced in this book. Any omissions will be rectified
in subsequent printings if notice is given to the publisher.

Warning!

Never touch wild animals or their homes. Some wild animals carry diseases. Scared animals may peck or scratch you, especially if they are protecting a nest. Never feed seagulls by hand, go near a seagull's nest, or touch seagull droppings.

Note about spotter icon

Your eyes, ears, and nose can tell you if a seagull is nearby. Look for these clues as you read the book, and find out more on page 22.

Contents

Some words are shown in bold, **like this**.
You can find them in the glossary on page 23.

Who Has Been Spotted Stealing Food?

Gray and white feathers. Webbed feet. A hooked beak. It's a seagull!

You don't need to visit the seaside to see seagulls.

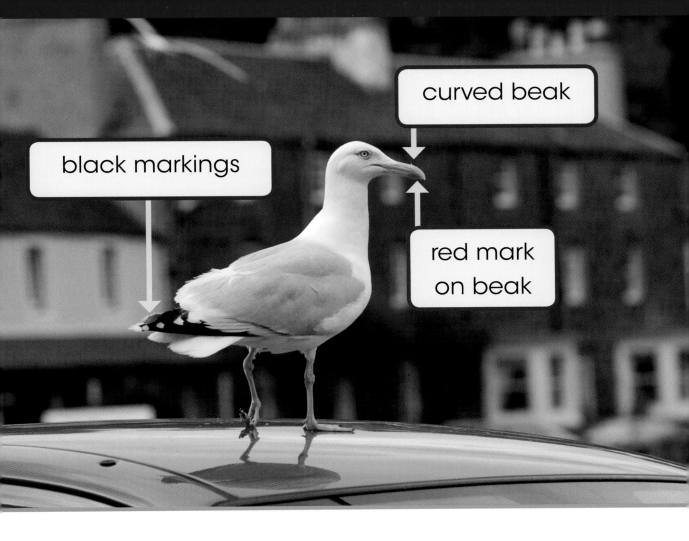

curved beak

black markings

red mark on beak

They like to live in towns and cities, too.

Come on a city safari. Find out if seagulls are living near you.

Why Do Seagulls Live in Towns and Cities?

In the past, seagulls only lived near coasts.

There are fish and sea animals to eat, and cliffs to build nests.

Seagulls can find everything they need in towns and cities, too.

There are safe places to build nests. There is also food that humans leave behind.

What Makes Seagulls Good at Living in Towns and Cities?

Seagulls are very smart.

That makes them good at learning to live in new places.

Seagulls are bold and do not mind being close to people.

They can fly well and escape from danger quickly.

Where Do Seagulls Rest?

Seagulls like to **roost** and **loaf** in groups.

Some choose high places, such as roofs, away from dangers on the ground.

Others choose wide, open spaces, such as playing fields, parking lots, and runways.

This means they can see danger coming.

What Do Seagulls Eat?

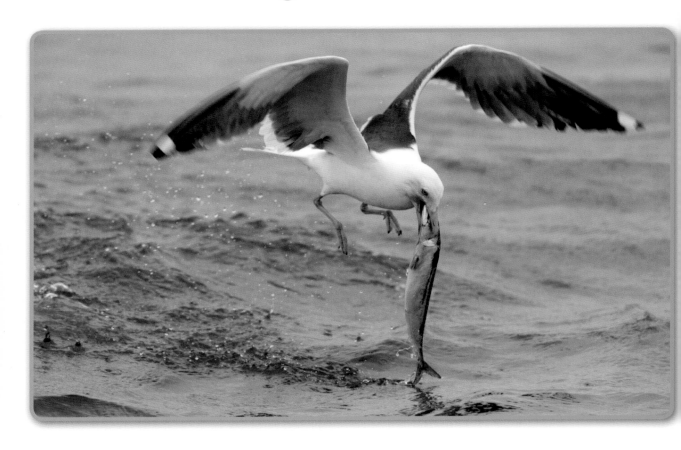

Seagulls eat seeds, grains, and fruit, but they prefer meat.

They dive out of the sky to grab insects, worms, and fish.

Seagulls are good at **scavenging** for food.

They eat anything they find, such as bird eggs, **roadkill**, and even baby seagulls.

Why Do Seagulls Like Living Near People?

Towns and cities are full of food that people throw away.

Flocks of seagulls fight over scraps in streets and parks.

Seagulls even steal food from people and pets.

They can help keep cities clean by eating dead animals and litter.

What Problems Do Seagulls Cause in Towns and Cities?

Not everyone likes sharing a city with noisy seagulls.

Their droppings are messy. They can damage cars and buildings.

Seagulls that live near airports damage airplanes by flying into them.

People use spikes and nets to stop seagulls **roosting** or to scare them away.

Where Do Seagulls Lay Eggs?

Pairs of seagulls **mate** once a year.

They like to build nests in the same place every year.

They choose to nest in a different place from where they usually live and eat.

Both parents help collect food and keep the eggs warm.

Why Is It Hard to Spot Baby Seagulls?

Seagull chicks stay in the nest for several months.

Their parents chase away any person or animal that gets too close.

When the young seagulls leave the nest, they are almost fully grown.

You can spot them by looking for patches of brown feathers.

Seagull Spotter's Guide

Look back at the sights, sounds, and smells that tell you a seagull might be nearby. Use these clues to go on your own city safari.

1. Seagulls learn where to find food, and keep coming back. They can make a mess by raiding cans and ripping open trash bags.

2. Seagulls make loud mewing and wailing calls. Large **flocks** can be very noisy.

3. Droppings show you where seagulls like to perch, **roost**, and nest.

4. If you see a seagull swooping down to attack someone, it is probably protecting a nest. Seagulls call loudly to scare people and animals away. If that doesn't work, they might peck and scratch.

Picture Glossary

 flock group of birds eating, resting, or flying together

 roadkill dead animal that was killed crossing a road

 loaf rest or sit around without doing anything

 roost settle down to rest or sleep

 mate when a male and female animal get together to have babies

 scavenging looking for food that has been thrown away or left over

Find Out More

Books

Metz, Lorijo. *Discovering Seagulls.* New York: Rosen, 2012.

Thomas, Isabel. *Brilliant Birds.* Chicago: Raintree, 2013.

Web sites

FactHound offers a safe, fun way to find Internet sites related to this book. All of the sites on FactHound have been researched by our staff.

Here's all you do:
Visit www.facthound.com
Type in this code: 9781432988104

Index